HUMAN BODY BASICS

The cells in your body contain a structure called DNA, which you inherit from your parents.

For living things there are seven life processes: breathing, feeding, growing, moving, feeling, reproducing and excreting. Living things with all of these characteristics are classed as organisms. You are an organism, and so are oak trees, octopuses, orangutans and otters.

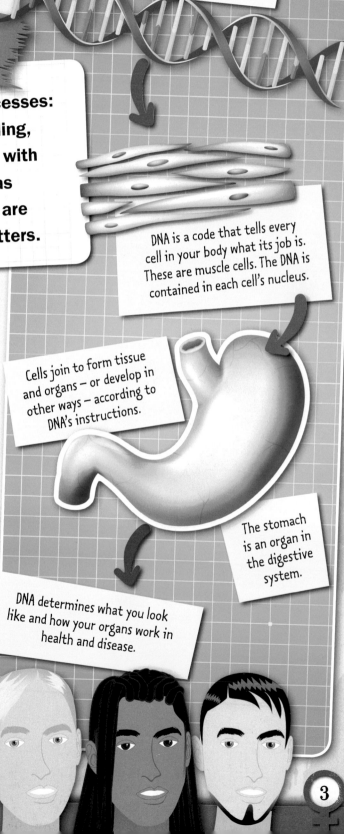

DNA is a code that tells every cell in your body what its job is. These are muscle cells. The DNA is contained in each cell's nucleus.

Cells join to form tissue and organs – or develop in other ways – according to DNA's instructions.

The stomach is an organ in the digestive system.

DNA determines what you look like and how your organs work in health and disease.

Smallest parts

The smallest part of each organism is a cell. All cells have the same basic parts but the structure changes depending on the job the cell does. You have trillions of cells in your body, and hundreds of different types. Cells are so small that they can only be seen using a microscope.

Tissue and organs

Cells of the same type can join together. These groups of cells are called tissue. One type of tissue can join with another type, or a combination of types, to form organs.

Body systems

There are many organs in the body with particular jobs to do. They work together in systems, such as the circulatory system or the digestive system. Body systems take care of the seven life processes.

A NEW HUMAN

What does your birthday mean to you? For most people, it means presents, perhaps a party, and hopefully everyone making a fuss and being nice to you. But have you ever really thought about what your birthday IS? It's a celebration of the exact day when you – a new human – entered the world.

The cycle of life

On your birth day, your journey through the world began. Human lives go from babyhood through infanthood to childhood, then into puberty, adulthood and, finally, old age. All living organisms – not only humans – go through this cycle of growing up and getting old before they die.

Humans are sometimes said to pass through seven stages of life: babyhood, infanthood, childhood, adolescence, adulthood, middle age and old age.

Although a person's 'birth day' is the day they entered the world, a human life actually starts about nine months earlier than that. It begins when a single cell from a man's body joins with a single cell from a woman's. The two cells fuse into a new cell, and create something that grows and develops, until it eventually becomes a person!

China had the largest population in the world, at 1,355,692,576 in July 2014.

STRANGE BUT TRUE!

A baby's teeth start to form six months before it is born. Few babies are born with actual teeth, though — only about one baby in 2,000, in fact.

Billions of birthdays

Of course, having a birthday isn't all that unusual. There are over 7 billion people in the world, and every single one of us has a birthday. People die each year, but overall people are living for longer, and more people are born than die. This means that the world's population is getting bigger all the time. In fact, each MINUTE it increases by 158 people.

DON'T TRY THIS AT HOME!

Have you ever noticed that people often look like their mum or dad? The first scientist to work out that characteristics are always passed on from generation to generation was Gregor Mendel. He did it by spending years (from 1857 to 1864!) growing thousands of pea plants. Mendel watched how characteristics, such as pod shape or colour, were passed on over the years in the seeds of the plants.

It was the 1950s before scientists discovered DNA, which is what actually passes on the characteristics. Without Mendel's patient pea growing, they might not have known what to look for!

WHAT MADE YOU ...YOU?

You are one crazy, mixed-up kid. Don't worry, though – it's not ONLY you. We're *all* mixed-up. It's because we are all made of a mixture of things we inherited from our mum and dad. Our height, hair colour and other characteristics all come from our parents.

The same, but different

No one looks 100% like either of their parents. Instead, we are all a jumbled-together mixture of both of our parents. The way the ingredients mix together is what makes people individuals – rather than exact copies.

Siblings often look similar to each other, and similar to their parents. But they won't all look exactly alike. Although the parents are the same, the way their characteristics combine is a little different each time they have a baby – so each baby looks a bit different from the last.

STRANGE BUT TRUE!

DNA is a code that determines how your body will develop. It is contained in all your body's cells, except mature red blood cells.

DNA affects your hair and eye colour, which hand you write with, your height, and all the other factors that make you an individual.

Each strand of DNA is the shape of a spiralling ladder. This shape is called a double helix.

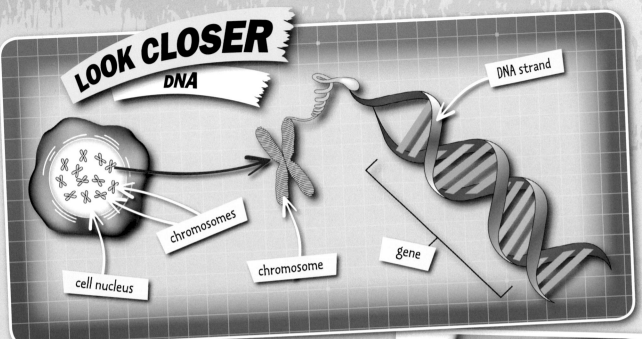

DNA strand

chromosomes

chromosome

gene

cell nucleus

Genetics

The science of how we inherit characteristics from our parents is called genetics. Genetic characteristics are passed on by DNA (short for deoxyribonucleic acid). The strands of DNA in your body's cells are like an instruction list, telling them how to grow and develop. Your DNA comes from both of your parents' DNA. Their instruction lists got mixed together, making a completely new one for you.

Our genes can pass on good things, such as being skilled at sports or having great hearing. They can also sometimes pass on bad things, for example poor eyesight, or heart problems.

Anyone who has children passes on some of their characteristics to the future through their genes. Those characteristics will still be around long after the human who passed them on has died.

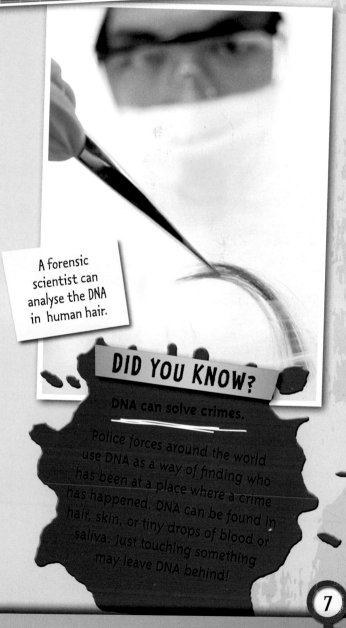

A forensic scientist can analyse the DNA in human hair.

DID YOU KNOW?

DNA can solve crimes.

Police forces around the world use DNA as a way of finding who has been at a place where a crime has happened. DNA can be found in hair, skin, or tiny drops of blood or saliva. Just touching something may leave DNA behind!

THE START OF YOUR STORY

The life of every human being begins when a sperm cell from a man combines with an egg cell inside a woman – a process known as fertilisation. This meeting is the end of a very competitive race for the sperm cell. There isn't just one sperm trying to meet up with the egg – there are between 6 and 150 million!

Sperm cells race towards an egg cell.

Expert swimmers

It's a good job that some sperm are expert swimmers. When the race starts, though, they have just begun to swim for the first time! Inside the man's body, the sperm can't swim at all. Their swimming skills only activate as they leave.

There is only ONE winner in the sperm race. Once a single sperm has burrowed into the egg, the egg's outer wall changes and no more sperm can get through.

STRANGE BUT TRUE!

Before the science of fertilisation was discovered in the late 1800s, some people thought that humans came pre-formed, contained within the tiny head of a sperm. These 'spermists' claimed that women's bodies just provided a place for the sperm to grow.

A fertilised cell

Together, the sperm and egg contain all the DNA code for a new human. Scientists do not know exactly what determines which sperm gets in, but once it is inside, the egg is fertilised. The fertilised cell follows the DNA's instructions and divides. The cells divide again and again, creating a cluster of cells that roots itself in the mother's womb, or uterus. The cells continue to divide and change, forming an embryo.

STRANGE BUT TRUE!

Whether you are a boy or a girl was decided at the moment when the sperm and egg that formed you combined.

Your sex was decided by the combination of chemicals called chromosomes in the sperm and egg that made you. Eggs always contain the X chromosome, but sperm can have X or Y — therefore it is the sperm that determines the sex of the baby.

LOOK CLOSER
CELL TO EMBRYO

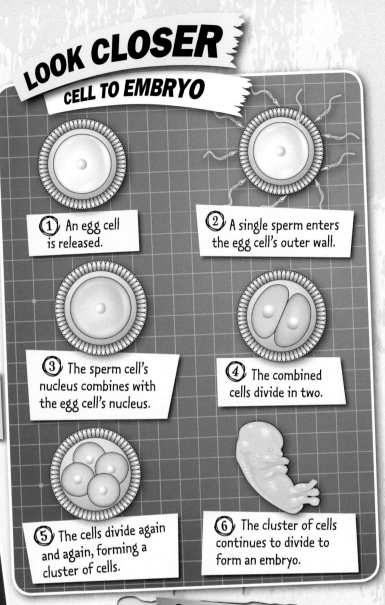

① An egg cell is released.

② A single sperm enters the egg cell's outer wall.

③ The sperm cell's nucleus combines with the egg cell's nucleus.

④ The combined cells divide in two.

⑤ The cells divide again and again, forming a cluster of cells.

⑥ The cluster of cells continues to divide to form an embryo.

DID YOU KNOW?
Not all sperm are top swimmers.

Among sperm, the best swimmers have a rounded head, a neck section behind, and a wriggly tail that they use for swimming. Sadly, studies have shown that most sperm do not reach this ideal standard. Common problems include:

✳ a tiny head (or even two!)

✳ a bent neck that stops them swimming in a straight line

✳ a bent, broken or coiled tail (or even more than one), which makes swimming almost impossible.

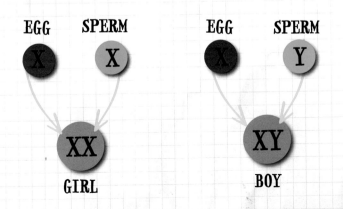

EGG   SPERM   EGG   SPERM

X   X   X   Y

XX   XY

GIRL   BOY

FROM CELL TO HUMAN

Once the embryo is around eight weeks old, it becomes known as a foetus. Over the coming weeks and months its limbs and organs continue to form and grow, until it is ready to enter the world.

Waste products are also carried away through the umbilical cord. The placenta grows at the same time as the foetus. By the final weeks of pregnancy, the placenta is 2–3cm thick and as big as a large dinner plate.

The growing foetus

The foetus grows inside a sac of amniotic fluid. This keeps the foetus at a comfortable temperature, and cushions it from bumps and knocks. The foetus also drinks (and then wees out) amniotic fluid – so it's a good job the mother's body renews the fluid every three hours or so!

To grow, the foetus needs oxygen and nutrients. It gets these from the placenta – a temporary organ that grows inside the mother. Nutrients and oxygen flow from the mother's blood supply to the foetus through the placenta, and along a tube called the umbilical cord.

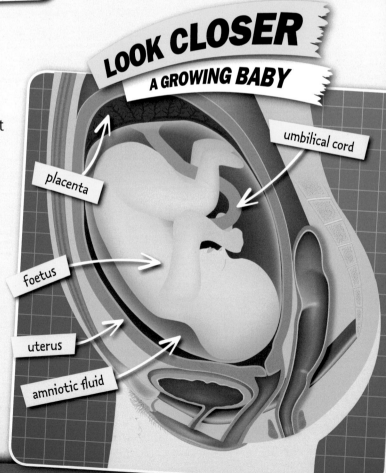

LOOK CLOSER
A GROWING BABY

umbilical cord

placenta

foetus

uterus

amniotic fluid

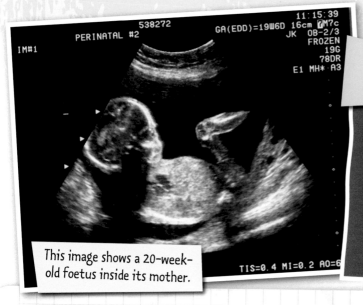

This image shows a 20-week-old foetus inside its mother.

STRANGE BUT TRUE!

In Bolivia, women rarely knit while they are pregnant. This is because knitting while pregnant is traditionally thought to cause the baby's umbilical cord to wrap around its neck.

Note: Knitting does not *actually* cause this!

A growing embryo or foetus changes and develops every day. Some of the key stages in the development inside the mother include:

AT FOUR WEEKS

There are just two layers of cells that have developed from the first two cells. Even so, these cells contain all the information needed to develop into a human and the amniotic sac that protects the embryo!

AT EIGHT WEEKS

At eight weeks the growing embryo becomes known as a foetus. The baby's arms and legs grow longer and hands and feet start to develop.

AT 12 WEEKS

At 12 weeks, the arms and legs are long and thin, and the head is about half the baby's size. The baby is around the size of a kidney bean, and has tiny webbed fingers!

AT 24 WEEKS

The baby's lungs are developing, along with its taste buds. The baby is now around 25cm long.

AT EIGHT MONTHS

The foetus is almost ready to be born. Even though it does not breathe inside the mother, the brain, lungs and other organs are well formed.

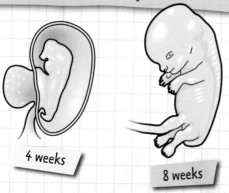

4 weeks

8 weeks

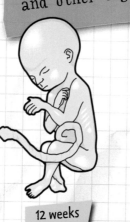

12 weeks

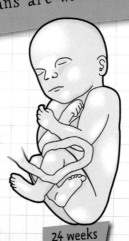

24 weeks

INTO THIS WORLD

After nine months of growing inside the mother, most babies are ready to come out into the world. In fact, babies NEED to come out. Their escape route to the outside is already a tight fit. If they carry on growing inside their mother for much longer, they might not fit through!

Being born

Being born usually takes about eight hours if it is the mother's first baby, though it can take 18 hours, or even longer! Second births often happen more quickly. There are three separate stages to being born:

1 Contractions

First, the muscles in the mother's abdomen automatically start to contract then relax. The contractions, called labour, happen more and more often, and become more powerful. They slowly push the baby out through a tiny opening, called the cervix, at the bottom of the uterus. Luckily it widens to help!

LOOK CLOSER

GIVING BIRTH

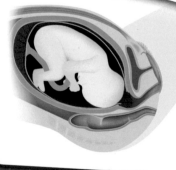

CONTRACTIONS

BIRTH

AFTERBIRTH

DON'T TRY THIS AT HOME!

Around the world there are lots of unusual newborn-baby customs.

✳ In Finland, there's been a tradition for the last 75 years of babies sleeping in cardboard boxes.

✳ Swedish babies are sometimes left outside in the cold (wrapped up and in a pram), to help them resist illnesses later in life.

✳ In Bulgaria, some people think making a fuss of a new baby makes the Devil want to steal it. If you REALLY want to fool the Devil, you spit in the baby's eye!

② Birth

The baby squeezes down the birth canal and starts to come out head first. Its mother helps by deliberately using muscles inside her body to push the baby out. Finally, it is born.

③ Afterbirth

Babies are born with their umbilical cord still connected to the placenta. Within a few minutes this is cut. Within an hour, the placenta also comes out of the woman's body. The birth is over.

STRANGE BUT TRUE!

Your tummy button shows where the umbilical cord connected you to your mum. People have different shaped belly buttons depending on what the cord was like, and how and where it was cut.

STRANGE BUT TRUE!

Babies have a soft gap between the skull bones, to allow the skull to be flexible and compress in the narrow birth canal during birth. The protein that stops a baby's skull from hardening until after it has been born is called 'noggin' — which is also a slang word for 'head'.

Early birds

Babies that are born early are called premature babies, and need specialist care. Most babies that are born a month early survive as their organs are well formed. Even babies born two months early can survive, though some may experience health problems as they grow up.

DID YOU KNOW?

Caesar gave his name to a way of being born.

Some babies cannot be born in the normal way. They may be too large, or positioned at the wrong angle. When this happens, a small cut is made in the mother's abdomen and uterus to deliver the baby.

This is how the Roman emperor Caesar was once thought to have been born. Today, the operation is often called a caesarian or C-section birth.

TWINS:
TWO TYPES

Most women give birth to a single baby. Sometimes, though, a woman gives birth to not one but TWO babies. These are called twins. If *three* babies arrive at once, they are called triplets. The record for the number of babies all born at once is eight. They were born in 2009, in California, USA.

Are all twins the same?

No, there are two different types of twins:

✳ **Identical twins** look almost exactly alike when they are young. As they grow up, though, things like their diet and how much exercise they do affect what they look like. Even when they do exactly the same things all the time, the twins begin to look slightly different.

✳ **Non-identical** twins are born at the same time, but do not look the same even when they are young.

What causes the two types of twins?

Twins develop in two different ways, which decide whether they are going to be identical or non-identical:

✳ **Identical twins** are the result of a fertilised egg (see page 9) splitting and becoming two embryos. Because they come from a single egg and sperm, the embryos have exactly the same DNA. They grow up looking confusingly alike!

Identical twins start life looking exactly alike. When they get older, it may still be hard to tell them apart.

identical twins   non-identical twins

A town called Cândido Godói, in Brazil, claims to be the 'twins capital of the world'. Between 1959 and 2008, 8% of births resulted in twins — compared to 1% in the rest of Brazil.

Cândido Godói has a rival, though. Among the Yoruba people of Nigeria, it's claimed that three of every 19 births results in twins. That means over 15% of births produce twins.

DID YOU KNOW?

Having twins runs in families (sometimes).

If a woman's mother or grandmother ever had non-identical twins, she is about four times as likely to have twins herself. This is because she may have inherited the possibility for her body to produce two eggs at the same time.

Having identical twins is different. It does not seem to run in families, so having identical twins is pure luck.

✳ **Non-identical twins** develop when a woman's body produces two eggs at the same time. Each embryo is formed by a different egg and different sperm, so they have different DNA. They grow up looking alike, but only as alike as brothers and sisters.

STRANGE BUT TRUE!

About a quarter of identical twins are a type called 'mirror-image twins'. One is right-handed, the other left-handed. Their fingerprints are also mirror images.

Non-identical twins Scarlett and Hunter Johansson

15

BEING A BABY

After a baby has been born, it still has a LOT of growing up to do. For example, a baby cannot see clearly straight away. Its brain is not yet fully developed. In fact, the brain – and a lot of the rest of the body – carries on developing until the 'baby' is in its 20s!

Changing babies

Lots of big changes happen during a baby's first year of life. The bones in the skull, hips and some other parts of the body knit together. The muscles become stronger and control of movement becomes better. At the same time, vision and hearing both improve.

New skills

As a baby's body develops, so does its brain. This means that most babies are able to learn lots of new skills during their first year:

✳ Talking

Babies start imitating noises very early in their lives. By the time they are six months old, many know basic sounds such as 'ma' or 'ba', but few learn the actual meaning of words before their first birthday.

✳ Moving around

Newborn babies make small, jerky movements. As their muscles develop and become stronger, their movements become more controlled. Their first lessons are to hold their heads up themselves, and to roll over. During their first year, most babies progress through sitting up to crawling around, and start to pull themselves up to standing.

STRANGE BUT TRUE!

Babies grow really quickly! In fact, it's a good job they eventually slow down. If an average-sized baby carried on growing at the same rate as in the first year, it would be 7.6m tall and weigh nearly 140kg by the time it was 20 years old!

✳ Thinking things through

To begin with, babies don't think much about what they are doing. They cry when they are hungry or cold or have done a poo in their nappy. As their brains develop, babies steadily become better at working out the world around them. They start to recognise familiar voices or the sound of their own name.

Babies' brains develop quickly during their first year of life.

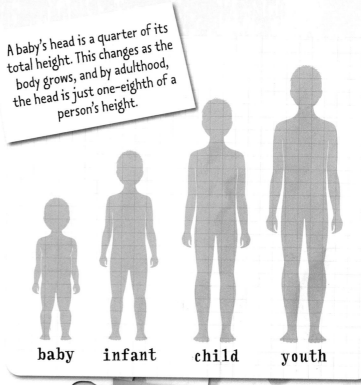

A baby's head is a quarter of its total height. This changes as the body grows, and by adulthood, the head is just one-eighth of a person's height.

baby   infant   child   youth

DID YOU KNOW?

Almost all babies are born with blue eyes.

Babies' eyes (like everyone's) contain a chemical that changes colour when it is exposed to sunlight. If a baby has a lot of this chemical, its eyes go brown, or even sometimes black, after it is born. If a baby has very little of the chemical, its eyes stay blue.

The exceptions to this rule are albino people, whose bodies do not contain the chemicals that colour most people's eyes, skin and hair.

Almost all babies start life with blue eyes, but only about 10% of adults have them.

17

FROM TODDLING
TO CHILDHOOD

When a baby learns to walk, people usually call it a 'toddler'. The name comes from the fact that they 'toddle' at first – meaning they can't walk very well. Once a baby starts to walk, it usually gets good at it very quickly. Toddlers learn lots of other new skills as they grow into childhood.

Talking

From baby noises, children start making sounds that you can recognise as words. Toddlers start to learn to speak some time between their first and second birthdays. They can join words together to say simple things like, 'Carry me'. After their second birthday they start learning more and more words each day: about 10 a day until they are six, then up to TWENTY a day until they have reached a point where they can communicate easily.

LOOK CLOSER
BRAIN DEVELOPMENT

The brain's structure changes and a child learns new things.

9 MONTHS

2 YEARS

4 YEARS

Moving around

Once babies can stand up, they want to get moving. They start walking with support as they gain balance and coordination. Once they can walk, toddlers start picking things up and carrying them around – a good way of developing strength! By the time they are two, most children can run, and enjoy jumping and climbing. By their third birthday, few children have to think about walking or running at all – they just do it automatically.

They need a little help at first, but most babies have learned to walk by the time they are 18 months old.

DID YOU KNOW?

At birth, human brains are similar to chimpanzees'.

When it is born, a baby's brain is very similar to the brain of a young chimpanzee. But then the baby's brain puts on a massive growth spurt, and develops far ahead of any chimp! It doubles in size by the baby's first birthday. Between birth and three years old it grows faster than at any other time, and uses about 60% of the baby's energy.

Thinking things through

Some time after their first birthday, toddlers start to work out problems. For example, they know to go to a cupboard and get a toy, even though they cannot see the toy. Their brain's ability to think things through keeps growing, until by the time most children are seven they can understand the rules of games (or bedtime, or school). By the time they are 12, they can explain the reasons for the rules, solve problems, and are able to think about events from other people's points of view.

STRANGE BUT TRUE!

Mammals such as humans, monkeys and gorillas need to be cared for by their parents for a long time after birth. It is years before a human baby, for example, would be able to run away from predators!

Other mammals, such as horses, cows, hippopotamuses, dolphins and whales, are better equipped for life in the wild. They can walk or swim just hours after being born.

GROWING UP: PUBERTY

BRILLIANT BODY FACT

Puberty makes young people clumsy! (They do get over it.)

After childhood, the next big change to a young person's growing body happens when puberty begins. Puberty is the physical change from childhood to adulthood. This is the time when a person becomes able to have children of his or her own.

When does puberty begin?

Puberty can start at a variety of ages. Girls often begin puberty at 11, but can be anything from eight to 14 years old. Boys are usually about a year behind: the average age to start is 12, but they can be anything from nine to 14. Puberty usually lasts for three years in girls and four years in boys, but it can be longer or shorter than this.

What happens during puberty?

When puberty arrives, chemical messengers called hormones start zinging around a person's body. In boys the most important hormone is testosterone. In girls, it is oestradiol. These hormones trigger the growth of adult sex organs (see pages 22–25) and cause other changes to the body.

Changes in boys

Boys' voices change, and get deeper. They begin to grow dark body hair, particularly on their armpits and pubic area. Boys often grow rapidly taller and their muscles develop.

DID YOU KNOW?

Puberty genes

Scientists have discovered that the start of puberty is triggered by two genes. One has the dull name of GPR54. The other has the brilliant name of KiSS1.

One day, KiSS1 suddenly starts producing special chemicals called kisspeptins. These cause GPR54 to turn on (until now, it has been inactive). GPR54 starts a chain reaction in your body, and puberty begins.

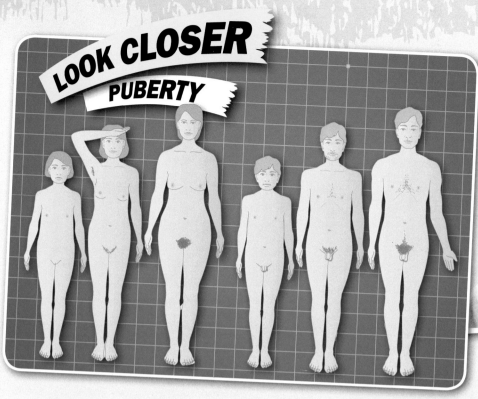

Spots are an unwelcome part of puberty for some young people.

Changes in girls

Girls' bodies start to look like an adult woman's: breasts form, their hips widen and their muscles develop. Their pubic hair grows, and they begin to have periods (see page 23 to find out more about these).

Once puberty is finished, a person's sex organs are fully developed.

Puberty problems

The changes to your body that happen during puberty can bring some problems. These include spots, which are caused by your skin releasing more oil; body odour, which happens because new sweat glands grow in your armpits, feet and pubic area; and sudden changes of mood, caused by the hormones your body is releasing.

DON'T TRY THIS AT HOME!

The artist Leonardo da Vinci (1452–1519) was famous for his accurate drawings of human anatomy — particularly what people looked like on the inside. However, this wasn't quite the case with his drawings of women's bodies, which are said to look more like those of animals. Experts think this was because no one would let Leonardo have female bodies to dissect!

FEMALES AFTER PUBERTY

When a female has finished puberty, her sex organs are fully formed and her body is capable of having children. Once her ovaries begin releasing egg cells, she may become pregnant if she has sexual intercourse.

✳ **The uterus** is the space where the foetus grows when a female becomes pregnant. Normally the uterus is the size of a grown-up's fist – but it has to be able to stretch enough for a baby to fit inside. The uterus can expand by as much as TWENTY times when a woman is pregnant.

Female sex organs

A female's sex organs are made up of two key parts:

✳ **The ovaries** are two storehouses for egg cells. From each ovary, a passage called a fallopian tube leads to the uterus.

Each month a single egg is released from the ovaries – it is thought they take it in turns. Each female starts life with hundreds of thousands of egg cells, but the number decreases as they get older. By the time females are old enough to have children, most have about 34,000 egg cells. Only about 400 of these will ever be released.

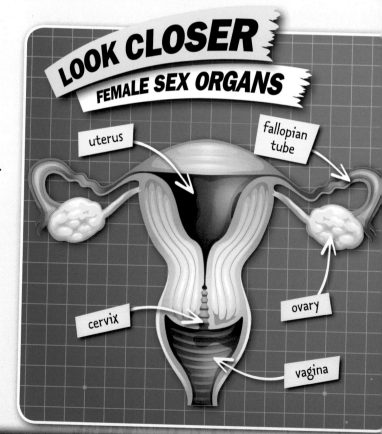

LOOK CLOSER
FEMALE SEX ORGANS

uterus

fallopian tube

cervix

ovary

vagina

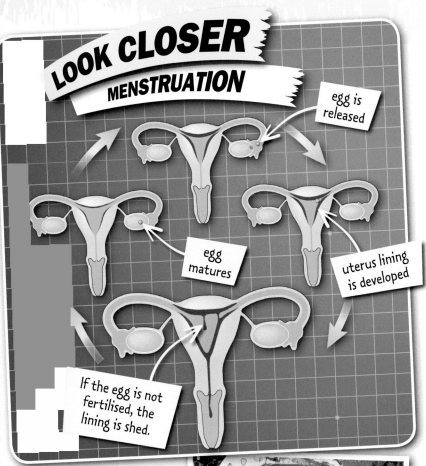

egg is released

egg matures

uterus lining is developed

If the egg is not fertilised, the lining is shed.

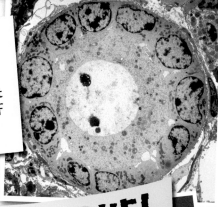

This magnified view shows a cross-section of an ovary follicle – the site where mature eggs are released. At the centre is the nucleus of the developing egg.

At the bottom of the uterus is the cervix, a ring of muscle. The cervix is connected to the outside world by a tube called the vagina. At the opening to the vagina are four folds of skin, called the labia.

The menstrual cycle and periods

A female can only become pregnant if an egg has been released by her ovaries. For most women, this happens roughly every 28 days. Each loop of 28 days is known as the menstrual cycle.

As a woman's ovary release an egg, the lining of her uterus thickens. If she becomes pregnant, this is where the embryo will bed in. If she does not, after a few days the thickened lining comes off. It leaves her body, along with blood and mucus, though the vagina. This is called a period.

STRANGE BUT TRUE!

In the past, people have come up with some odd theories about menstruating women: Ancient Roman historian Pliny the Elder claimed that a menstruating women could stop hailstorms, lightning, and whirlwinds; he also claimed that if she walked around a field of corn, all the bugs would fall off the plants. Science today, says there is no connection between menstruating women, and the weather or crops.

DID YOU KNOW?

Women may have inspired the first calendars.

Many women have a menstrual cycle of 28 days. Some researchers think that this cycle may have been behind the first calendars developed by humans.

MALES AFTER PUBERTY

Once puberty is finished, a male's sex organs are fully developed. He is able to produce sperm, which are made and stored in the testicles. If he has sexual intercourse, his sperm can cause a female to become pregnant.

Testicles

One of the changes that happens to a male during puberty is that his testicles become able to produce sperm. The testicles are two oval organs. The average adult testicle is roughly the same size as a large walnut in its shell, though not the same shape. Usually, the right testicle is a bit bigger than the left, and the left one hangs down a bit further.

Before birth the testicles are inside the male's body. Following birth, though, they descend into a hanging skin sac called the scrotum. They are here because the best temperature for sperm production is 1–2°C lower than human body temperature. If the testicles were inside, they would be too hot.

STRANGE BUT TRUE!

Most male mammals have a bone in their penises. The smallest belongs to the common shrew, whose penis bone is 0.5mm long. Humans, apes, bulls and horses are among the few mammals that don't have a penis bone.

a common shrew

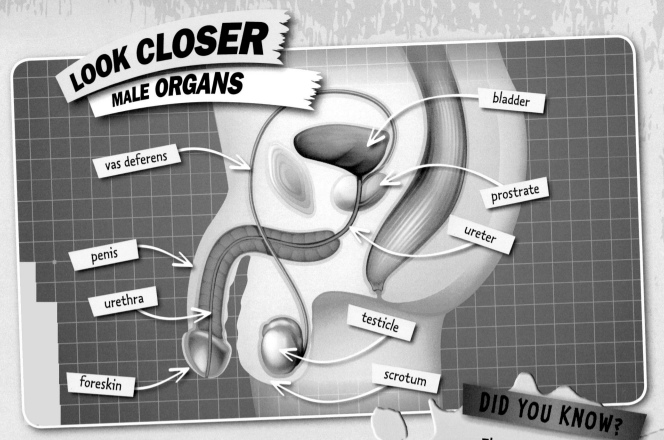

bladder

vas deferens

prostrate

ureter

penis

urethra

testicle

scrotum

foreskin

The penis

From the testicles, a tube loops up inside the body, then out again through the penis. The penis is used for both urination and reproduction. Males urinate through their penis via a tube, the urethra, leading from the bladder to the penis.

For sexual intercourse and reproduction to happen, the penis needs to become firmer and longer. To achieve this, some of its tissue fills with blood. This is called an erection.

STRANGE BUT TRUE!

Testicles have their own temperature control system. On a hot day, the scrotum hangs down loosely. This keeps the testicles out in the air, as far away from the body's heat as possible. On a cold day, the scrotum tightens up and brings the testicles closer to the warmth.

This magnified view shows a cross-section of a testicle, and the cells where sperm is produced.

GETTING OLDER

BRILLIANT BODY FACT

The oldest person to swim the English Channel was 73!

Your body does not stop developing after puberty. Your bones carry on getting stronger and your muscles get larger. Your vision, hearing and reaction times may improve as you reach your 20s. Most people reach their 'physical peak' – the time when their body is working as well as it ever will – in their 20s or early 30s.

Post-peak changes

Once a person has reached their physical peak, they should be able to stay there for many years. This depends partly on whether they eat well and do plenty of exercise. For example, someone who exercises regularly should be as strong at 50 as they were at 30. There are some changes, though, that happen to almost everyone:

LOOK CLOSER

BONE AND JOINT PROBLEMS

These two joint problems can affect anyone, but are most common among older people.

healthy joint

osteoarthritis joint

joint becomes less cushioned

Osteoarthritis causes pain in the joints.

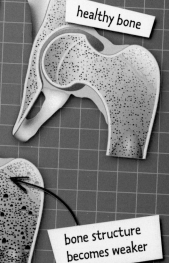

healthy bone

osteoporosis bone

bone structure becomes weaker

Osteoporosis causes bones to break more easily.

✱ In your 30s, hearing and eyesight usually start to get worse.

✱ In your 40s and 50s, your bones start to become less strong, and your heart is not able to beat as quickly. Women experience the menopause: the uterus lining stops forming and they no longer have periods; their body stops releasing eggs, and they can no longer have children. Men's bodies become less able to produce plenty of healthy sperm.

✱ From their 60s onwards, many people's physical and mental abilities noticeably decline. In particular, their memory gets worse, their joints become less flexible, and their heart and lungs are no longer able to work as hard.

These changes do not affect everyone equally. How we age is another part of being an individual. Two things decide how your body will decline as you get older: your genes and your behaviour. Find out more about both of these on the next page.

Tony Bennett

STAYING FIT AND HEALTHY

If you leave a bicycle out in the rain, never put oil on its chain, and just drop it on the ground when you get off, it won't last very long. But if you look after a bike, it lasts for years. Your body is the same. If you care for it, it works better and lasts for longer.

Lifestyle choices

How you live your life has a BIG influence on how well your body works when you are young, and as you enter old age. If you want to live to be healthy at 100 (or more), here are three key pointers:

Genetic influences

Your genes are the instructions that tell your body how to grow. You inherited them from your parents. A lot of what happens to your body as you get older is controlled by your genes. They influence everything, from whether a man goes bald to a person's chances of developing some diseases. At the moment, there is nothing you can do about your genes – so if your dad is bald, enjoy your hair while you have it!

✳ Eat well

As your body is growing, it needs the right kinds of nutrients to become healthy and as strong as possible. Eating the right foods makes sure your bones, muscles, brain and all the rest of you works as well as possible. Avoid eating a lot of fatty or sugary foods as they can cause health problems.

Vegetables and protein are key parts of a healthy balanced diet.

28

✳ Do exercise

People who exercise regularly live longer than those who don't. They are also able to do more, especially as they get older. But you do not have to wait until you are older to benefit from exercise. There's lots of evidence that getting fitter helps kids do better at school, too.

✳ Avoid things that are bad for you

Drinking alcohol, smoking cigarettes and taking drugs have all been shown to have a bad effect on people's bodies. They affect the brain, heart, lungs and other organs.

STRANGE BUT TRUE!

Even when he was an old man, former US President Harry S Truman was lively and full of energy. He claimed this was because every day, he walked a mile before breakfast.

DID YOU KNOW?

Genetic diseases may soon be curable.

Some diseases, such as breast cancer, seem to run in families. Today, scientists are working out which genes trigger these illnesses. In the future, they may be able to remove or adapt the gene to stop the illness happening.

Fauja Singh is said to be the world's oldest marathon runner – he began running marathons in his 80s and finally put away his race shoes at the age of 101.

GROWING WORDS!

abdomen part of the body containing your digestive organs, basically from the bottom of your ribs to your hips

albino a person or animal who does not have any colouring because they lack pigment in the body. Their skin is pale and their hair or fur is white, while their eyes are red.

anatomy the study of the structure and parts of the human body

cancer a disease in which cell multiplication is out of control. Some cancers eventually cause the body systems to fail.

chromosome a thread-like structure, made of DNA (genes), and contained in the nucleus of body cells

dissect to cut apart structures of an organism, to investigate its anatomy

DNA the genetic code that determines how your body will develop. DNA is contained in the nucleus of body cells, and is inherited from your parents.

fertilisation the moment when a female egg and a male sperm combine

flexible able to bend easily

hormone a chemical messenger, which triggers actions within the body

inherit to get from your parents

nutrients the substances needed by living things for nutrition, repair and growth

placenta an organ that grows temporarily on the lining of a pregnant woman's uterus. The placenta's job is to provide the baby with nutrition and oxygen, and to filter out waste.

pregnant when a female has an embryo or foetus growing inside her

premature early. Premature babies are ones that have been born sooner than is usual.

protein chemicals within the body, which do lots of different jobs. Among the most important jobs are triggering chemical reactions inside the body, protecting against sicknesses, carrying messages, and helping transport material around the body.

puberty the time when a person's body changes from child to adult, and they become capable of having children of their own

reaction time the time it takes to respond to something. At the start of a race, for example, someone's reaction time is the time from the starting signal going off to when they start running.

sexual intercourse the act that may lead to a female becoming pregnant. During sexual intercourse, the male's penis goes into the female's vagina, then releases sperm.

surgeon a doctor who specialises in doing operations, in which the patient is cut open so that their insides can be treated

urination weeing – the body's way of getting rid of some of its waste products

GROWING YOUR MIND

Would you like to grow more knowledge about your body and reproductive system? Here are some good places to find out more:

BOOKS TO READ

Truth or Busted: *The Fact or Fiction Behind Human Bodies*, Paul Mason, Wayland 2014

Go Figure: *A Maths Journey Through the Human Body*, Anne Rooney, Wayland 2014

Mind Webs: *Human Body,* Anna Claybourne, Wayland 2014

The World in Infographics: *The Human Body,* Jon Richards and Ed Simkins, Wayland 2013

WEBSITES

http://kidshealth.org/kid/grow/

This website is a really good place to find out about the human body. It has lots of articles on puberty and growing up.

http://www.childrensuniversity.manchester. ac.uk/interactives/science/exercise/

The Children's University of Manchester, UK, has all sorts of information for kids, presented in the form of labelled illustrations. You can start finding out about the effects on your body of regular exercise.

PLACES TO VISIT

In London, the **Science Museum** has regular exhibitions about how the body works. The museum is at:

Exhibition Road
South Kensington
London SW7 2DD

The Science Museum also has a good website, with information about the human body, including loads of fascinating facts, here:

www.sciencemuseum.org.uk/whoami/findoutmore/ yourbody.aspx

The **Natural History Museum** has an amazing 'Human Biology Gallery' where you can get a taste of anything from what a human baby experiences while still inside its mother, through how senses like hearing and smell operate, to the jobs your blood does for you. The museum is at:

The Natural History Museum
Cromwell Road
London SW7 5BD

The museum also has a website with a human biology section.

http://www.nhm.ac.uk/visit-us/galleries/blue-zone/human-biology/

INDEX

WAYLAND

Published in paperback
in 2016 by Wayland
Copyright © Wayland, 2016
All rights reserved.

Editor: Annabel Stones
Designer: Rocket Design (East Anglia) Ltd
Consultant: John Clancy, Former Senior
Lecturer in Applied Human Physiology
Proofreader: Susie Brooks

Dewey Number: 612.6-dc23
ISBN: 978 0 7502 9251 1
Library ebook ISBN: 978 0 7502 9250 4
10 9 8 7 6 5 4 3 2 1

Wayland, an imprint of
Hachette Children's Group
Part of Hodder & Stoughton
Carmelite House
50 Victoria Embankment
London EC4Y 0DZ

An Hachette UK Company
www.hachette.co.uk
www.hachettechildrens.co.uk
Printed in China

Artwork: Stefan Chabluk:
p7 t, p9 t, p11 b, p23 t.

Picture credits: Getty Images: p15 br The Washington
Post / Contributor, p29 br Jeff J Mitchell / Staff;
Science Photo Library: p7 cr, p15 tl JACOPIN, p17
bl PIXOLOGICSTUDIO, p18 JACOPIN, p21 tl PETER
GARDINER, p23 cl STEVE GSCHMEISSNER, p25 bl
STEVE GSCHMEISSNER; Shutterstock: p3 t, p3 ct, p3
cb, p3 b, p4 tr, p4 br, p5 t, p5 cl TonyV3112, p5 br,
p6 l, p6 br, p8, p10, p11 t, p12 cl, p12 b, p13 cr, p14,
p17 tr, p17 br, p19 tl, p19 tr, p19 br, p21 tr, p21 bl,
p22, p24, p25 t, p26 l, p26 r, p27 s_bukley, p28, p29
cl, p29 tr.
Graphic elements from Shutterstock.

CONTENTS

Y G
G Y

KIN

reproductive system

FIND OUT HOW YOUR BODY WORKS!

Paul Mason

WAYLAND